WORLD RELIGIONS

ISLAM

Khadijah Knight

Thomson Learning
New York

Words appearing in *italic* in the text have not fallen into common English usage. The publishers have followed Merriam Webster's Collegiate Dictionary (Tenth Edition) for spelling and usage.

First published in the United States in 1995 by
Thomson Learning
New York, NY

Published simultaneously in Great Britain by Wayland (Publishers) Ltd.

U.S. copyright © 1996 Thomson Learning

U.K. copyright © 1995 Wayland Publishers Ltd.

Library of Congress Cataloging-in-Publication Data
Knight, Khadijah.
  Islam / Khadijah Knight.
    p.   cm.—(World religions)
  Includes bibliographical references (p.   ) and index.
    ISBN 1-56847-378-8
    1. Islam—Juvenile literature. I. Title. II. Series:
  World religions (Thomson Learning (Firm))
  BP161.2.K56   1995
  297—dc20   95–30445

Printed in Italy

Cover: This boy from Bukhara, Uzbekistan, is keeping alive the traditions of Islamic scholarship by studying the Koran.
Title page: Jumeira, Dubai, mosque at night.
Contents page: Even children join in the Id prayer in Cairo, Egypt.

Acknowledgments

The author and publishers thank the following for their permission to reproduce photographs: Guy Hall: 38 (top); Christine Osborne: *cover, contents page,* 24, 27, 34; TRIP: *title page* (H. Rogers), 4, 5 (top) (Joan Wakelin), 5 (bottom) (S. Hill), 6, 7 (J. Kilby), 9 (J. Kilby), 10 (top) (H. Rogers), 10 (bottom) (A. Gamiet), 12, 15 (H. Rogers), 17, 18 (M. Barlow), 19 (top), 19 (bottom) (A. Gamiet), 22 (C. Rennie), 23 (F. Good), 25, 28 (H. Rogers), 29, 31 (H. Rogers), 32, 33 (top) (W. Jacobs), 33 (bottom), 35 (H. Rogers), 37 (M. Lines), 38 (bottom), 39, 40 (top), 40 (bottom) (C. Rennie), 41, 45 (top) (H. Rogers), 45 (bottom).

Contents

Every time a Muslim
mentions Muhammad,
he or she adds, "*Salla-
llahu alaihi wa sallam*"
("Peace and blessings of
Allah upon him"). In
print, these Arabic
words are expressed by
this logotype: ﷺ.

After the names of all
the prophets and the
names of the twelve Shia
imams (see page 11),
Muslims add "Peace be
upon him." These words
in Arabic, "*Alaihi
salaam*," are represented
by the logotype ﷺ.

INTRODUCTION

I slam is the faith and way of life of more than a
billion people around the world. These followers of
Islam are called Muslims, and the basic belief that they
declare is "There is no god except Allah and
Muhammad is the Messenger of Allah." These words
are called the *Shahadah*.

To help get ready for salah (prayer), *this young boy in
Peshawar, Pakistan, spreads extra prayer mats in the
courtyard of the mosque.*

Muslims believe that, without Allah's guidance,
human beings are not fully able to understand the
meaning and purpose of life. They believe that, from
the beginning of creation, over a long period of time,
Allah sent messengers to earth to help people worship
the one true God and to show them how to follow a
"straight path" in their behavior. The first of these
messengers, or prophets, was Adam ﷺ. The final messenger was the prophet Muhammad ﷺ, who lived in
Arabia in the sixth to seventh centuries C.E. (Common
Era; see page 47).

Muslims believe that Allah's message was revealed to
Muhammad ﷺ, in Arabic, by the angel Jibril (Gabriel).
It was Allah's final guidance for people everywhere and

4

at all times. Allah's own words were spoken to Muhammad ﷺ, and these were written down to form the Koran, which is the Muslim holy book. The Koran must never be changed. Muslims around the world learn to recite the Koran in Arabic, whatever their mother tongue.

It is written in the Koran:

> Allah invites to the abode of peace, and leads whom He wills to a straight path. (Koran 10:25)

This means that anyone can choose Islam as his or her faith, at any stage of his or her life. There are Muslims of all races and nationalities and from greatly diverse backgrounds. They are all united by their belief in the *Shahadah* and by certain basic practices that Muslims everywhere must follow. The worldwide community of Muslims is called the *Ummah*.

Muslim young people on their way home from school in Sarawak, Malaysia

A mosque in Mostar, Bosnia, now destroyed by the fighting. Millions of Muslims live in former Yugoslavia.

5

S L M

The Arabic language is based on root words made up of consonants. For example, the consonants *S L M* form the root that means "peace."

The terms *Islam*, *Muslim*, and *salaam* come from that root.

Islam is the state of peaceful obedience to Allah's guidance.

A **Muslim** is someone who believes in and accepts Allah's commands and is at peace with himself or herself and with everything in creation.

As-salamu alaykum (Peace be upon you) are the words Muslims use to greet one another.

The Shahadah, *written above the entrance to a mosque in Istanbul, Turkey*

Muslims must follow these practices. They help them to be more aware of Allah in everything they do.

Saying the *Shahadah* in Arabic: *"La ilaha illa-Llah, Muhamadur rasulu-Llah,"* and so declaring their faith in the oneness of Allah and in the prophet Muhammad ﷺ as His final messenger.

Communicating with and worshiping Allah five times each day, in the way that Muhammad ﷺ taught. This is called *salah*. Prayers are recited in Arabic.

Fasting from before dawn until sunset every day during the Islamic month of Ramadan. This fasting is called *sawm*.

Paying an annual welfare levy of 2.5 percent of what wealth remains after personal and business expenditure. This is called *zakah*.

At least once in one's lifetime, going on a pilgrimage to Mecca, Mina, Muzdalifah, and Arafat, from the 8th to the 13th of the Islamic month of Dhul Hijjah. This pilgrimage is called hajj.

Muslims believe that this life is a trial in preparation for *akhirah*, the hereafter. On the Day of Judgment, they will be asked to account for their actions in this life, which the angels have recorded. Therefore Muslims try to lead purposeful and active lives, although they believe that Allah has the final control over what will happen to them.

1
THE STORY OF ISLAM

Allah's messengers

Muslims trace the roots of Islam to Adam ﷺ, the first man. They believe that he was the first of a large number of prophets. For Muslims, prophets were people sent by Allah to teach humankind how to behave toward all that He had created and how to worship Him as the one true God.

The prophet Ibrahim ﷺ lived four thousand years ago in the Middle East. He taught that it was useless and wrong to worship idols. It is written in the Koran that Ibrahim ﷺ and his son, Isma'il ﷺ, built *Bayt Allah* (the House of Allah) in Mecca and invited everyone to worship there. Another name for this building is the Kaaba, which means "cube-shaped."

Twenty-five of the prophets sent by Allah to humankind are mentioned in the Koran. Many of them are also found in the Torah and the Bible (the books of the Jewish and the Christian religions). Some of them are Ibrahim ﷺ (Abraham), Isma'il ﷺ (Ishmael), Musa ﷺ (Moses), Dawud ﷺ (David), and Isa ﷺ (Jesus).

Today the Kaaba is within the grand mosque in Mecca. The mosque has been extended many times to make room for the growing numbers of pilgrims.

IBRAHIM TEACHES AGAINST IDOL WORSHIP

"Behold," he said to his father and his people. "What are these images to which you are so devoted?"

They said, "We found our fathers worshiping them."

He said, "Indeed you have been in plain error—you and your fathers... and by Allah, I will certainly plan against your idols..."

So he broke them to pieces, all but the biggest of them...

They said, "Who has done this to our gods?...Are you the one that did this with our gods, O Ibrahim?"

He said, "No. This was done by this biggest one! Ask them, if they can talk."

Then they were confounded with shame; they said, "You know full well these idols do not speak!"

Ibrahim said, "Do you then worship, beside Allah, things which can neither be of any good to you nor do you harm?...Have you no sense?"
(Koran 21:52-67)

Muslims believe that, as time went by, Ibrahim's teachings were forgotten. Allah sent more Prophets, but always people eventually ignored some of their teachings or changed them to suit themselves.

The prophet Muhammad ﷺ

Muslims believe that the prophet Muhammad ﷺ is the final prophet. He was born in the city of Mecca in 570 C.E. At this time people had forgotten the one true God. They had filled the Kaaba with idols and were making money from pilgrims who came there.

Muhammad ﷺ used to go away from the bustle of the city to spend time quietly alone, contemplating, in a desert cave. One night while he was there he suddenly heard the angel Jibril instruct him, "Proclaim."

"Proclaim, in the name of your Lord and Cherisher, who created man from a clot of blood. Proclaim and your Lord is Most Bountiful—He who taught the use of the pen taught man that which he knew not." (Koran 96:1-5)

At first he was afraid, but when the angel had said the same words three times, he realized that he should repeat and learn what he was being told. This revelation introduced Muhammad ﷺ to his new way of life as a prophet of Allah. For the next 23 years, he continued to receive the revelations that contain Allah's guidance (the Koran) and to proclaim Allah's final message.

The Dome of the Rock in Jerusalem encloses the rock from which Muhammad ﷺ ascended into the heavens on Laylat ul-Miraj. *It is a place of pilgrimage for Muslims.*

Laylat ul-Miraj, the "Night Journey" of the prophet Muhammad ﷺ, was a miraculous event that affects the daily life of Muslims to this day. According to the Koran, on this night the Prophet ﷺ was taken by the angel Jibril from the mosque in Mecca to Mount Moriah in Jerusalem. Here he led all the prophets in

LAYLAT UL-QADR

Muhammad ﷺ received the first revelation of the Koran on one of the last ten nights of the month of Ramadan. Muslims commemorate it most often on the 27th night of Ramadan. They call it *Laylat ul-Qadr,* the "Night of Power."

"The Night of Power is better than one thousand months. Therein come down the Angels and the Spirit by Allah's permission on every errand: Peace!... this until the rise of morn!" (Koran 97:3-5)

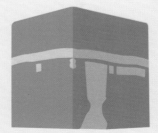

Muslims must pray five times a day. At each of these times, all Muslims thank Allah for His mercy as they journey through life.

prayer. Then he traveled up through the heavens until he reached the very throne of the Creator. Allah in his mercy revealed to him the order for five obligatory times of prayer (*salah*) every day and night.

Medina and its Islamic laws

Many people in Mecca were angry when Muhammad ﷺ told them to behave fairly and not to worship idols. They persecuted him and planned to kill him.

Some people in Yathrib, to the north of Mecca, asked Muhammad ﷺ to become their leader and to settle rivalries between tribes that were upsetting their community. Muhammad ﷺ moved to Yathrib in 622 C.E., and it became known as Madinat-un-Nabi (City of the Prophet), or Medina.

To stop the fighting between tribes, Muhammad ﷺ drew up laws to make sure that everyone was treated fairly and equally. These laws were revolutionary

The Prophet's Mosque in Medina has been extended many times to allow more Muslims to offer salah *inside.*

because until this time people had been loyal only to their own tribe or family. News soon spread of how the laws worked to help people and, before the prophet Muhammad ﷺ died in 632 C.E., the city of Mecca and many other places in Arabia had agreed to be ruled by Islamic laws.

Sunni and Shiites

After the death of Muhammad ﷺ, his companion Abu Bakr was chosen by some to lead the community. Others believed that the prophet ﷺ had wanted Ali ؓ, his cousin and son-in-law, to be his successor. Those who felt this became known as the *Shi'at Ali* (Party of Ali), or Shiites. The rest became known as *Ahl-as-Sunnah wa-l-Ijma* (the people of the custom of the prophet and the consensus), or Sunni.

Abu Bakr was succeeded as *khalifah* by Umar. (The word *khalifah*, which means successor, is often rendered as caliph in English.) After Umar came Uthman and eventually Ali ؓ. The death of Ali ؓ in 661 ended the line of "rightly guided" successors and the division between Sunni and Shiites became more marked. Sunni Muslims did not believe that the *khalifate* should pass only to the family of the prophet ﷺ. They wanted to be able to elect their leaders. The Shiites felt that the sons of Ali ؓ and grandsons of Muhammad ﷺ, Hassan, and Hussein ؓ had inherited the spiritual and political leadership of the community.

Yazid, a later *khalifah*, demanded the loyalty of Hussein ؓ, but Hussein ؓ would not accept him. In 680 Yazid sent an army of four thousand men to fight against Hussein ؓ, who was traveling with his family and supporters. They were massacred, but two of his sons survived and the Shia system of spiritual leadership, known as the imamate, passed on through them. Most Shiite Muslims believe that there have been twelve infallible imams, and that the last of these did not die but will come back to restore justice on earth.

When Sunni Muslim societies have tried to live entirely by Islamic law, they have also tried to bring back

Every person would be treated equally. No matter how rich or important their families, all people would receive the same justice.

If people were poor or in need they would be helped by money collected from taxes.

The Jewish people in Medina would be free to practice their religion without interference.

If anyone attacked Medina, all of its citizens would join together to defend one another.

the system of the *khalifah*, to lead the community. Many Muslims believe that what is needed today is strong religious and political leadership from a good and scholarly *khalifah*. Although they disagree strongly on some things, both Shiite and Sunni Muslims still use the same Koran, follow the example of the prophet ﷺ, and share Islamic beliefs.

The spread of Islam

In the hundred years after the death of the prophet Muhammad ﷺ, Islam spread as far as north Africa and central Asia. These areas had been occupied and ruled by the Roman, Byzantine, and Persian empires, which were unpopular because of their warring and heavy taxes. The people did not resist the Muslim conquerors and even supported them against their previous rulers.

The golden gates to the mosque of Imam Hussein ﷺ in Kerbala, Iraq. Imam Hussein ﷺ was martyred here in 680 by the armies of Yazid. In the twentieth century, this important place of Shia pilgrimage was devastated by the armies of Sadam Hussein, president of Iraq.

When the Christian city of Damascus in Syria surrendered to the Muslim leader Khalid ibn Walid in 635 C.E., its bishop brought Khalid food. Khalid promised the inhabitants "security for their lives, properties, and churches...As long as they pay a fair tax, nothing but good shall befall them." This story illustrates how Khalid ibn Walid tried to set a good example of Koranic teaching.

By the ninth and tenth centuries, Baghdad was the greatest city in the expanding Islamic world. Through contact with China, people in Baghdad had learned the art of papermaking. This encouraged the production of books, and knowledge of Islam spread.

Islam became established in India in 711 C.E. By the sixteenth century India was ruled by the Mogul Empire. Since most people in India were Hindus, one of the Muslim emperors, Akbar, made a Hindu his second in command. He also ordered Muslims not to kill cows, which Hindus consider sacred.

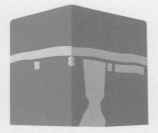

KEY DATES IN THE HISTORY OF ISLAM

BEFORE THE COMMON ERA

In the beginning   The prophet Adam ﷺ is created.

2000   The prophets Ibrahim ﷺ and Isma'il ﷺ build the Kaaba in Mecca.

1200   The prophet Musa ﷺ is given the Taurat (Torah) by Allah.

1000   The prophet Dawud ﷺ is given the Zabur (Book of Psalms) by Allah.

COMMON ERA

1st century   The prophet Isa ﷺ is born.

570   The prophet Muhammad ﷺ is born in Mecca in Arabia.

610   The prophet Muhammad ﷺ receives the first revelation of the Koran.

622   The prophet Muhammad ﷺ migrates to Medina and establishes the first Islamic state. This is counted as the beginning (year 1) of the Islamic calendar.

632   The prophet Muhammad ﷺ dies in Medina.

632 - 661   The period of the *khalifahs*. After the death of the prophet ﷺ, Abu Bakr became the first *khalifah* to lead the community. In Sunni tradition he is followed by Umar, Uthman, and Ali.

632 - early 10th century   The period of the imams. In Shia tradition, spiritual and political leadership of the community passed from the prophet ﷺ to the twelve imams through his cousin Ali ﷺ.

680   The martyrdom of Imam Hussein ﷺ at Kerbala, Iraq.

711   Muslims enter Spain and begin Islamic rule.

750 – 850   The *Shari'ah* (the Islamic system of law) is developed.

970   The Islamic University of al-Azhar is founded in Cairo, Egypt. It is the world's oldest university.

1138 - 93   Lifetime of Salah ud-Din, Governor of Egypt, adversary of Richard the Lion Heart, and victor in the Crusades. Salah ud-Din is a model of Islamic chivalrous behavior.

c.1300   Osman, who gives his name to the Ottoman dynasty, begins to establish his power in Turkey.

KEY DATES IN THE HISTORY OF ISLAM

1453	The Ottomans conquer Constantinople, capital of the Byzantine Empire, and rename it Istanbul. The Ottoman Empire expands and by the 1520s it includes southeast Europe (including most of Hungary), the Middle East, and north Africa.
1492	Muslim rule in Spain ends.
1550	A Muslim kingdom is established in Sumatra. From here, Islam spreads to Java, the Moluccas, and Borneo. In the seventeenth century there is a "golden age" of Islam in Indonesia.
1798	Egypt, under Muslim rule since 672, is occupied by France.
1809	Usman dan Fodio founds the *khalifate* of Sokoto in Nigeria.
1827	Great Britain, France, and Russia support Greece against its Ottoman rulers.
1830	The French invade Algeria.
1873	The Dutch attack the Sumatran Muslim kingdom.
1882	The British attack and occupy Alexandria, Egypt.
1915	The Constantinople agreement between Great Britain, France, and Russia on the division of Ottoman lands.
1917	The British fight the Ottomans for control of Gaza in Palestine.
1922	The end of the Ottoman Empire and *khalifate*.
1927	The Persian shah abolishes Islamic dress and rules that all men must wear European-style clothes and hats.
1954	The Algerians rebel against French colonial rule.
1950s - 60s	Muslims migrate to Europe, the United States, Australia, and throughout Arabia.
1979	The Persian shah is deposed and the Islamic Republic of Iran is established.
1990s	Wars in Bosnia, Myanmar, and Chechnya kill thousands of Muslims.

ISLAM IN SPAIN

In 711 C.E. a Muslim army of North African Berbers (a nomadic people) landed in Spain and gained control of a large part of the country. Europeans called them the Moors.

In the tenth and eleventh centuries, Córdoba, the capital of Muslim Spain, became the most splendid city in Europe. There were streetlights, many houses had running water, and there were hundreds of public baths. Very few people in Europe at this time could read or write; however, in Muslim Spain there was primary education for all, so nearly everyone became literate. Most of

the education was based in the seven hundred mosques in Córdoba, and lectures were given there. Advances were made in medicine, science, astronomy, music, and book classification in libraries. Scholars from other parts of Europe came to study under great masters such as ibn Rushd and ibn al-Arabi.

Inside the Great Mosque in Córdoba, famed for its beautiful arches

From India, Islam spread through Muslim missionaries and traders to southeast Asia, Malaysia, Indonesia, and the Philippines. One attraction of Islam was its followers' belief in the equality of all people. This was also a reason for the spread of Islam to the west African countries of Mali, Senegal, Nigeria, and Ghana between the eighth and the eighteenth centuries.

Because Islam encourages its followers to learn about Allah's creation, cities under Muslim rule became centers of learning. Timbuktu in Mali grew up around its mosque. Its students opened Koran schools throughout west Africa, which continue teaching Islamic studies today.

15

THE OTTOMAN EMPIRE

When the Ottomans captured Constantinople in 1453, their leader, Sultan Mehmet II, renamed the city Istanbul. To help it develop, he invited Muslims and Jews who were suffering persecution in Spain and other parts of Europe to make their homes there. In 1560 the Sulmaniyyah mosque complex was completed, including the mosque, seven colleges, a hospital, an asylum, a soup kitchen, a bathhouse, schools, stores, a sports ground, and fountains.

The empire expanded to rule much of the Islamic world. Everywhere, roads and rest houses for travelers were built, and there was an efficient system of legal and social services.

However, at the beginning of the nineteenth century, the empire came under pressure. Austria and Russia took much of its northern territories, and France, Great Britain, and Russia made a treaty to help Greece against the Ottomans. In 1918, at the end of World War I, France, Great Britain, Russia, Holland, and Italy ruled nearly all of the countries of northwest and east Africa, the Middle East, India, and southeast and central Asia.

Europe and the Islamic world

The European colonial powers imposed their own legal and social systems on their colonies in place of the existing Islamic ones. Many Muslims in the colonies were taught that European systems were better than those of Islam, about which they were able to learn very little.

Since the colonies gained their independence in the latter part of the twentieth century, Muslims there have been trying to reestablish the teachings and institutions of Islam.

As a result of the connections made between Europe and the Islamic world, many Muslims have settled in Europe. There are also increasing numbers of converts to Islam; Muslims today make up the second largest religious group in Europe. They are maintaining the teachings and practices of Islam, building mosques, and joining in activities and work that benefit the whole community.

2

THE WORLD OF ISLAM

There are many Muslims worldwide, as the map on pages 20-21 shows. Wherever Islam becomes established, it accepts cultural customs that are not in conflict with Islamic teaching.

This chapter looks at the experience of Muslims in three very different parts of the world: Iran, the United States, and central Asia.

Iran

Iran is a big country, slightly larger than Alaska. Ninety-eight percent of the population are Muslims, most of whom are Shias.

In 1979 Shia Muslims established the Islamic Republic of Iran. Its leader is a Shia ayatollah (sign of Allah)—that is, someone who has studied Islamic theology and law to a very high degree at one of the renowned religious colleges in Tabriz, Qumm, or Mashad.

These colleges take students from all over the world. They may progress from being a mullah (scholar) to *hujjat-ul-Islam* (proof of Islam), and at that stage they may be invited by existing ayatollahs to join their ranks. The ayatollahs are greatly respected for their knowledge and ability to make religious and legal decisions.

The huge scale and beautiful craftsmanship of this mosque in Isfahan reflect the Islamic understanding of the power and magnificence of Allah.

A mullah in a mosque at Isfahan. Spending time in quiet prayer and concentration is part of his spiritual training before he is able to teach others.

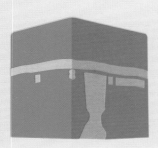

The government also includes an elected parliament, the *majlis*. It is working to make sure that the teachings of Islam are followed in all areas of life.

Beautiful mosques were built in Isfahan and other cities in Iran, during its "golden age" of Islam in the seventeenth century. The books of some of the most famous poets and mystics of Islam are kept in the library of rare books and ancient Korans in Mashad.

African-American Muslims

Most African-Americans today are descendants of more than 10 million west African Muslims who were taken as slaves to America in the seventeenth and eighteenth centuries. The slave masters disregarded the Africans' own religions and cultures and converted them to Christianity.

Fifty years after slavery was abolished, African-Americans became interested in Islam. In 1914, Noble Ali Drew gave his followers Muslim names and taught them about the prophet Muhammad ﷺ. He gave them identity cards that said they were "Moorish Americans," in memory of the north Africans who had conquered Spain for Islam in the eighth century. He wanted them to shake off the identity forced on them by slavery.

In 1930, a man named Wallace Fard appeared in the poor areas of Detroit, saying that he had come from Mecca and that African-Americans were the "lost-found tribe of Shabazz." He named Elijah Muhammad to follow him as their next leader and, over the next 30 years, the Honorable Elijah Muhammad and growing numbers of followers set up schools, universities, and "temples of Islam." This new "Nation of Islam" helped start many black-run businesses and encouraged women and girls to train for jobs. People were taught to stay away from alcohol, drugs, and cigarettes, to have self-respect, and not to trust white people.

In the 1960s, Malcolm X became the spokesperson for the Nation of Islam. He became well-known in the civil rights movement, and white Americans grew fearful of the influence and power of the Black Muslims.

Malcolm X left the Nation of Islam and in 1964 made the Hajj (pilgrimage) to Mecca. This gave him a new understanding of Islam and, on his return to the United States, now named Al Hajj Malik al Shabbaz, he began to teach that Islam gives equality to all, black and white.

Today, crowds of African-American Muslims gather for Id *prayer in Washington Monument park in Washington, D.C.*

> America needs to understand Islam, because this is the one religion that erases from its society the race problem. Throughout my travels in the Muslim world.... I have...seen sincere and true brotherhood practiced by all colors together...

Such words made many people uneasy; Malcolm X was assassinated by extremists in his own group. But his ideas took root. By the 1980s, most of the two million African-American Muslims followed the same teachings and practices of Islam as Muslims worldwide.

The clothing Muslim men wear when they go on Hajj makes them all look alike. Seeing everyone like this, without status symbols or titles, is a powerful reminder that all are equal before Allah.

MUSLIMS AROUND THE WORLD

There are Muslims living in almost every country on earth, totaling more than one billion.

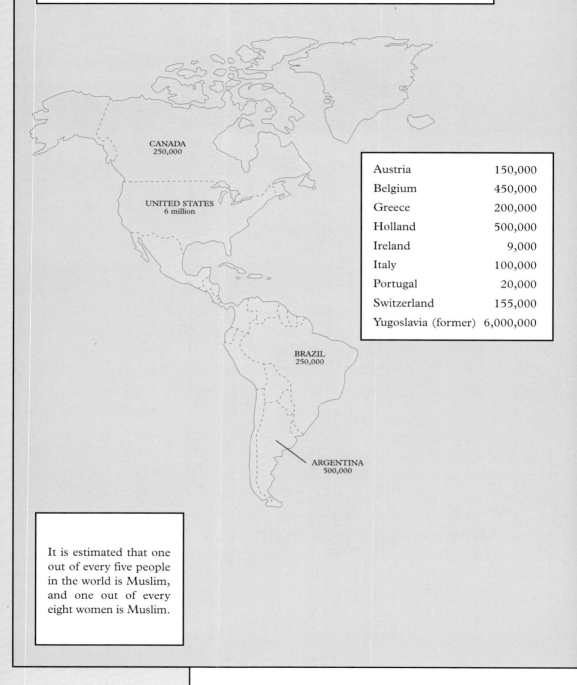

CANADA
250,000

UNITED STATES
6 million

BRAZIL
250,000

ARGENTINA
500,000

Austria	150,000
Belgium	450,000
Greece	200,000
Holland	500,000
Ireland	9,000
Italy	100,000
Portugal	20,000
Switzerland	155,000
Yugoslavia (former)	6,000,000

It is estimated that one out of every five people in the world is Muslim, and one out of every eight women is Muslim.

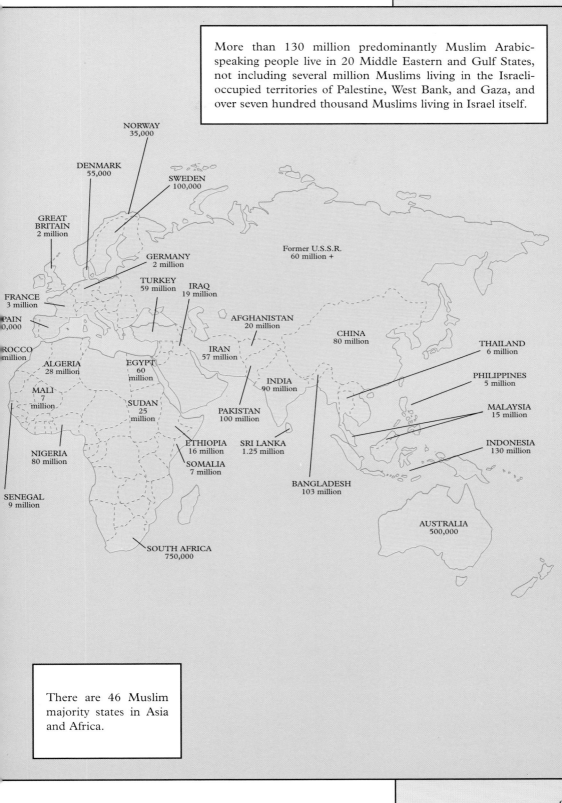

More than 130 million predominantly Muslim Arabic-speaking people live in 20 Middle Eastern and Gulf States, not including several million Muslims living in the Israeli-occupied territories of Palestine, West Bank, and Gaza, and over seven hundred thousand Muslims living in Israel itself.

NORWAY
35,000

DENMARK
55,000

SWEDEN
100,000

GREAT
BRITAIN
2 million

GERMANY
2 million

Former U.S.S.R.
60 million +

TURKEY
59 million

IRAQ
19 million

FRANCE
3 million

AFGHANISTAN
20 million

PAIN
0,000

CHINA
80 million

THAILAND
6 million

ROCCO
million

IRAN
57 million

EGYPT
60
million

ALGERIA
28 million

PHILIPPINES
5 million

MALI
7
million

INDIA
90 million

MALAYSIA
15 million

SUDAN
25
million

PAKISTAN
100 million

NIGERIA
80 million

ETHIOPIA
16 million

SRI LANKA
1.25 million

INDONESIA
130 million

SOMALIA
7 million

SENEGAL
9 million

BANGLADESH
103 million

AUSTRALIA
500,000

SOUTH AFRICA
750,000

There are 46 Muslim majority states in Asia and Africa.

21

Trade from the eastern Mediterranean to China helped spread Islam all along the Silk Route. Samarkand, in the heart of central Asia, developed as a remarkable and beautiful city.

In the fifteenth century its ruler, Ulugh Beg, built a huge observatory and wrote an encyclopedia about the paths and positions of stars. Land travelers across the central Asian deserts needed, like sailors, to navigate by the stars. It was also important for traveling Muslims to be able to determine the direction of *qibla* (see page 32) and the start of the lunar months.

Built in 1807, the Char Minar in Bukhara was the gatehouse to a madrasah *funded by a wealthy merchant.*

Islamic revival in central Asia

Fifty million Muslims live in five central Asian republics: Uzbekistan, Kazakhstan, Tajikistan, Kirgizia, and Turkmenia. These republics became self-governing in the early 1990s, after 70 years of Communist rule as part of the U.S.S.R.

From the late 1920s, people had been forbidden to practice or teach their faith. Many Muslims continued to learn the Koran and about Islam in secret. However, the mosques fell into disuse.

Before Communist rule, the city of Bukhara had 360 mosques. Now the people there are restoring the 120 mosques and *madrasahs* (Islamic schools and colleges) that are left, turning them from empty monuments back to busy places of worship and learning.

During Communist rule, only small official groups were allowed to go on hajj. "Now," says Jamila Nishan from Ashkabad in Turkmenia, "lots of central Asian Muslims will be able to visit the holy places of Islam and meet Muslims from all over the world."

3

SOURCES OF ISLAM

The Koran

Muslims sometimes call the Koran "our maker's handbook." They believe that the words in it are Allah's own words, exactly as they were revealed to the prophet Muhammad ﷺ. They also believe that the revelations made to Muhammad ﷺ were and are Allah's final guidance for people everywhere. The word *Koran* means "that which should be read."

With their Korans carefully wrapped, these girls in India go to learn how to read and pronounce the Arabic words of Allah's revealed book.

Allah's message was revealed to Muhammad ﷺ by the angel Jibril in Arabic at different times and in different places over a period of 23 years. Each year during the month of Ramadan, Muhammad ﷺ recited what he had been taught, to make sure that he had memorized it correctly. By the time of his death, all the revelations had been written down to form the Koran. Many Muslim men and women knew the whole Koran by heart.

HAFIZ

There are millions of people today who know the whole Koran by heart. They are called *hafiz*. The beautiful rhythmic language of the Koran makes it easy to memorize.

All Muslims learn to recite at least some short suras (sections), such as Al-Fatihah and Al-Iklaas, in Arabic so that they can perform their *salah* in the correct way. But often people read and study the Koran in their mother tongue. There are translations in many languages.

How the Koran is arranged

The Koran is arranged in 114 suras, and each sura consists of a number of *ayat* (signs).

The whole text is divided into 30 equal parts, for people who wish to read the complete Koran in daily sections over one month. It is also divided into seven equal parts, for people who want to read the whole Koran in one week.

Using the Koran

The Koran is recited by Muslims on almost every occasion in life, such as when remembering someone who has died or when giving thanks for success or a happy event. Many Muslims try to read a section of the Koran every day. Lots of people have pocket-sized copies with zipped plastic covers that they take everywhere and can read, for example, on the bus or the train.

Where books are expensive, as in Gambia, classes learn to read the suras from durable wooden boards.

AL-FATIHAH

Al-Fatihah (The Opener) is sura 1 of the Koran. Muslims recite it at least 17 times each day, during the 5 times of *salah*. It is also usually the first part of the Koran that Muslim children learn. Muslims think of it as the essence of the Koran and the Perfect Prayer, through which they offer worship and ask for guidance. It sums up their relationship with Allah.

In the name of Allah, Most Gracious, Most Merciful.
Praise be to Allah, Lord of the Worlds,
The Most Gracious, the Most Merciful;
Master of the Day of Judgment.
You alone we worship and You alone we ask for help.
Guide us on the straight way, the way of those You have favored,
Not the path of those who earn Your anger, nor of those who go astray.

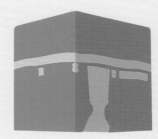

AL-IKLAAS

Al-Iklaas (which means "sincerity" or "purity of faith") is sura 112. It announces the most important idea in Islam, which is *tawhid*—the oneness of Allah. This sura says that polytheism, believing in lots of gods, is wrong and also that people should not try to picture Allah as a human being. This is usually the second part of the Koran that Muslim children are taught.

> In the name of Allah, Most Gracious, Most Merciful.
> Say: He is Allah the One.
> Allah, the Eternal and Absolute
> He begets not, nor is he begotten.
> And there is none like Him.

Hadith

The hadith are reports of the sayings and actions of the prophet Muhammad ﷺ, collected in the first century after his death. Each hadith comes with information about when the prophet ﷺ said the words, or did what he did and who heard or saw it. For example, Anas ibn Malik, who was employed by the prophet ﷺ as a servant, reported that the prophet ﷺ said:

The Kaaba (see page 7) has a beautiful cover embroidered in gold thread with words from the Koran.

> None of you truly believes until you wish for others what you wish for yourself. (al-Bukhari and Muslim)

Many scholars spent their lives making sure that everything written about the sayings and actions of the prophet ﷺ was true. They checked the honesty of everyone who gave a report. They considered whether the

THE SUNNA

All the customs and examples of the Prophet Muhammad's ﷺ behavior, reports of what he said and did, and stories about his life are called the sunna. The Hadith and *Sirah* (the prophet's ﷺ biography) are included in and considered part of the sunna.

The sunna is not in book form, like the collections of hadith and the biography. It is the totality of everything known about the prophet ﷺ. Together they are a source of guidance for Muslims about what to do and how to behave.

statement or action was reasonable, whether it matched the way the prophet ﷺ spoke, and whether it was in accordance with the teaching of the Koran. If they were satisfied, they accepted the report for their collection of hadith. Many thousands of hadith were accepted as true. Some of the most famous collections are Biharul Anwar, al-Bukhari, al Kafi, and Muslim.

Two other hadith are:

> Part of someone's being a good Muslim is leaving alone that which does not concern him or her. (Tirmidhi)

> If a believer plants a tree, or sows a field, and people and beasts and birds eat from it, all of it is charity on his/her part. (Muslim)

Shari'ah—*Islamic law*

In the eighth century, ways of understanding and interpreting the Koran and sunna were developed by scholars who founded the main schools of Islamic law. The Arabic word *shari'ah* means "a path to be followed."

Muslims believe that Allah is the ruler and judge of everything and everyone, and that human beings have the duty to care for everything Allah has created. The Muslim community uses Islamic law to try to uphold these beliefs.

Islamic law is able to deal with new developments, for instance in science, in a positive way. This is done by examining the Koran and sunna, applying reason, consulting knowledgeable people, and taking account of public interest. When the question of test-tube babies was considered in this way, the conclusion was that, as long as the egg to be fertilized and the sperm used were from the wife and husband of a married couple, the process was acceptable. It would not be acceptable to use either donor eggs or donor sperm.

---4---

HOME AND FAMILY LIFE

Muslims believe that the home should be a place of comfort where everyone can live, eat, and pray in an Islamic way.

It is Allah Who made your dwellings homes of rest and quiet for you. (Koran 16:80)

Calling the adhan *from a mosque in Cairo, Egypt*

Prayer

The five times of prayer, or *salah,* are determined by the position of the sun, so they vary from day to day through the year. In Islamic countries, the *adhan* (call to prayer) is made from the mosque to let everyone know that it is prayer time.

Muslim families in all countries usually offer their early morning and nighttime prayers together at home, and this helps everyone to learn and keep up their *salah.* Muslim homes have prayer mats and a space to pray. To keep the home, and especially the prayer

Prayer times vary by several hours depending on the time of sunrise and sunset every day.

Salat-ul-Fajr is prayed between the first light of dawn and sunrise.

Salat-ul-Zuhr is prayed after midday.

Salat-ul-Asr is the mid-afternoon prayer.

Salat-ul-Maghrib is the sunset prayer.

Salat-ul-Isha is prayed about an hour and a half after Maghrib.

Washing before salah

place, clean, many families leave their shoes at the front door.

Before *salah,* everyone washes in a special way called *wudu.* This means washing hands, mouth, nose, face, arms, head, ears, neck, and feet three times each in running water.

AN ISLAMIC HOME IN CYPRUS

Eleven-year-old Habiba Mustafa lives with her family in a traditional, old, Islamic-style house in northern Cyprus. The house is built around a beautiful flower-filled courtyard garden, watered from a central fountain. To the left and right of the main door are separate guest sitting rooms for men and for women. All the family's bedrooms, kitchen, and sitting rooms are on the far side of the courtyard. There is also a *hamam* or Turkish bathhouse, with a domed roof. The water tank for the *hamam* is heated by a fire.

Because Habiba's father is a scholar who teaches about Islam, many students come to visit and listen to his talks about the Koran and the sunna. Two large adjoining prayer rooms on the third side of the courtyard are used by the family and visitors for these occasions and for *salah.*

Even though their house is old-fashioned and made of mud bricks and wood, Habiba's mother likes it far better than her sister's modern apartment. "Our house is cool in the summer, warm in the winter, and is pleasant to live in," she says.

Mealtimes

At the beginning of a meal in a Muslim home, everyone says, *"Bismillah-ir Rahman-ir-Rahim,"* which mean "In the name of Allah All Gracious All Merciful."

As in all areas of their lives, Muslims try to follow the example of the prophet Muhammad ﷺ at mealtimes. It is part of the Sunna to offer food to guests and to share food made for family and religious celebrations with neighbors. If all the food, such as rice or couscous together with meat or vegetables, is served on one large plate, then it is considered good manners for each person to eat only from the part nearest to him or her, using the right hand.

No matter how delicious the food is, Muslims are taught not to eat hurriedly and not to be greedy and to make sure that everyone at the table has enough to eat. The prophet Muhammad ﷺ said that it was best for the stomach to be one-third full with food, one-third full with water, and one-third empty.

In Morocco, after each meal, a pitcher of water, a basin, and a hand towel are brought so that everyone can rinse his or her hands.

Food prepared for a feast in Kashmir. "So, eat of the sustenance Allah has provided for you, lawful and good; and be grateful for the favors of Allah." (Koran 16:114)

Food

What we eat and drink affects our bodies and health. Islam teaches that some things are good while others are harmful. Food and drink that Muslims are allowed to eat is called *halal*, which means "permitted." There are recipes for Muslim dishes from all over the world, but even hamburgers and sausages can be *halal*, provided that they are made with *halal* ingredients.

THE RAMADAN FAST

During Ramadan, Muslims eat and drink nothing during the hours of daylight. They have a predawn meal called *sahoor* and a meal called *iftar* to break the fast at sunset. Families prepare especially nourishing meals for *sahoor*. For *iftar*, people in north Africa have a thick soup called *harira*. The fast is broken in Arabia with dates and Arabic coffee; in Turkey, with olives and tea; and in India, with sweet, milky drinks and fruit.

Fasting reminds Muslims of how dependent people are on food to give them energy. Most of all it makes them aware of and grateful to Allah, who provides all food.

Muslims may eat:
> meat from any sheep, chicken, goat, or cow that has been killed by a butcher who says *"Bismillah Allahu Akbar"* ("In the name of Allah, Allah is Most Great");
> any edible vegetable or fruit;
> the eggs of *halal* birds.

Muslims may not eat or drink any of the following, which are *haram* (forbidden):
> the meat of pigs, including bacon, ham, pork, or any product made from pig;
> the meat of any animal, bird, or other creature that has died naturally or has been strangled;
> any reptiles, birds, or animals that are carnivorous;
> any kind of alcohol or food containing alcohol.

Some Muslims also do not eat shellfish.

HOME IN THE UNITED STATES

When Zeba Sadiq's family moved from Palestine to Colorado, they were the only Muslims in the area. There was nowhere to buy *halal* food, so they bought from the kosher grocery store. Zeba's mother bought meat, bouillon cubes, crackers, and other things there because she could be sure they would be free from any pork.

As the Muslim community in Colorado grew, stores opened to serve their needs. Now the Muslims have arrangements with local farmers to provide them with meat prepared under *halal* conditions.

One of Zeba's favorite meals is Bukhari rice. The recipe has been in her family for generations and is made with rice, meat, and homegrown carrots. Zeba is an avid gardener and thinks that Colorado carrots are the sweetest.

The roles of family members

Older family members follow the teachings and practices of Islam in all they do, and children learn from their example. There is an Arab saying that the mother is a school. Children are taught modest behavior, self-respect and respect for others, good manners, honesty, and consideration. They often learn to be charitable by sharing food with neighbors and people in need.

Fathers also have an important role. They must provide for their families to the best of their abilities. Within his home, a father is the imam for his family.

An understanding of responsibilities within the family is taken from the Koran and the sunna. Here are some examples:

With his sisters and little brother behind him, this young imam is practicing leading his family in salah.

> The right due to the child from its parents is for them to teach it writing, swimming, and archery ... and provide it with nothing but what is wholesome. (Hadith al-Bukhari)

> A man was sitting with the Prophet when his son came in. The man kissed him and sat him on his lap. Then his daughter came in and he let her sit down in front of him. The Prophet said: "Shouldn't you have treated them the same?" (*Sirah*)

> ...be kind to parents whether one or both of them reach old age in your life. Never speak badly to them but always speak to them with respect. And out of kindness, lower over them the wing of tenderness and say, "Oh my Lord, Have mercy on them as they cared for me when I was a child." (Koran 17:23)

31

5

COMMUNITY LIFE

QIBLA

The Kaaba in Mecca is the first house dedicated to the worship of Allah. To perform their *salah* as Allah has ordered, Muslims worldwide turn in the direction of Mecca. In the United States this means facing east.

This mosque in Brunei has lots of room for women to perform salah. *It was built in 1958, to the order of the sultan at that time.*

The mosque

Mosques can look very different from one another on the outside. In west Africa they may be made from mud; in China and Indonesia, from carved wood. In Iran and Turkey mosques are often covered in beautiful colored tiles. In Arabia many mosques are simply painted white. But inside, all mosques have the following:

a *mihrab*, an alcove in one wall, which shows the direction to face for prayer. This direction is called *qibla*.

if large enough, a *minbar*, a raised platform where the imam stands to speak to the people.

a prayer area for men, and often one for women.

Either inside or near it, every mosque has a place for people to wash to prepare for prayer. And many larger mosques have an open courtyard and a minaret, from which the *adhan* is called. In north Africa the minaret is traditionally a tall, square tower. In Turkey, it is narrow and round.

Before entering the prayer hall, people take off their shoes and either leave them on a rack or put them in a plastic bag to take with them. Inside there is no furniture; people stand, bow, kneel, and sit on their heels to worship. Very old people or those with disabilities may perform their *salah* sitting on a chair.

Mosques built from mud, like this one in Mali, stay refreshingly cool inside.

The imam

The work of the imam is to lead the five daily prayers, to give a talk at the midday Friday prayer, to perform marriages and funerals, to answer people's questions about Islamic teaching and practices, and to give advice to people about their problems. To lead men and women in *salah*, the imam must be a man, but a group of all women may choose a woman to lead their *salah*. Large mosques in towns and cities may have one or more full-time imams.

Other people at the mosque

Many other people work at important national mosques, including guides to

An intricately tiled and painted mihrab *in an old mosque in Bangladesh*

SALAT UL-JUMU'AH

Friday is the day of the week for Muslims to come together to pray the midday prayer and to listen to the *khutbah*, a talk by the imam about religious, topical, and practical matters. Most Muslims in non-Muslim countries are sad if, because of work or school, they or their children miss *Salat ul-Jumu'ah*.

This Muslim in Thailand is refreshing and preparing himself by washing before salah.

show visitors around. Some of these mosques have offices; libraries; bookshops; classrooms for *madrasahs*, where children and adults are taught the Koran; halls for weddings, lectures, and community events; and kitchens from which food is provided, especially in Ramadan. One office job is to distribute *zakah*, the welfare tax that all Muslims who can afford to must pay each year. The mosques also employ someone to prepare dead bodies for burial.

The jammah

Generally, the men, women, and children who use the mosque all share the work of running it. This local community is called the *jammah* and has the following responsibilities:

> to meet once a week for *Salat ul-Jumu'ah* and *khutbah*;
> to make sure that, when they have sufficient resources, no one among them is struggling in poverty or hardship;
> to settle any disputes that occur in the community;
> to try to help the community in the areas of Islamic education, health, and social and moral welfare.

The prophet Muhammad ﷺ said: "The Muslim community is like a single body. When one part is afflicted the other parts feel pain and fever" (Hadith Muslim).

A *jammah* can begin with a few Muslims who live or work in the same district coming together to find a place to hold the Friday prayer. They may use part of someone's home, store, or office for *salah* and as a *madrasah*, until they can save up for larger accommodation.

AN IMAM IN HOLLAND

Ahmad Patishuwissa is an imam in Ridderkerk, a small town in Holland. The community he leads has built a beautiful little mosque in a modern design. The families of many people in his *jammah* came originally from Indonesia in Southeast Asia and Suriname in South America. Because of marriages and the Dutch people who have accepted Islam, the *jammah* is multiracial.

Ahmad teaches the Koran to adults and children on three evenings per week and on Saturday mornings. He also leads the Friday prayer and all the *Id* celebrations. His family says that his work doesn't stop there. His daughter, Kerima, says, "People often come to our house to ask my dad's advice and get his help with all kinds of things, from money problems to health worries. If he can't help them himself, he usually knows someone who can."

The ummah

Muslims believe that they belong to a worldwide community called the *ummah*, or Nation of Muhammad. It is not important that they were born in different countries and have different customs; what matters is that they are all united as one community by their belief in Islam. Muslims are pleased that the *ummah* is made up of people of all races, without any distinction between them.

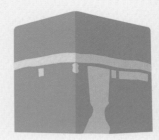

> Mankind. We created you from a single pair of a male and a female,
> And made you into nations and tribes, that you may know each other.
> (Not that you may despise each other.)
> (Koran 49:13)

35

6

NAMES

Muslim parents prefer to name their children after a good person or to choose names with good meanings.

Many boys are named after Allah's prophets: for example, Ibrahim, Idris, Ilyas, and Muhammad.

Other popular boys' names refer to the qualities of Allah. An example is Abdul Karim, which means "slave of the Bountiful." It would be wrong to call someone Abdul ("slave of") on its own. It would also be wrong to call someone just Karim, because that is Allah's name.

Girls are often named after women in the family of the prophet Muhammad ﷺ, such as his daughter, Fatimah Zahrah, and his wife, Khadijah.

A MUSLIM LIFETIME

All important events in a Muslim lifetime, such as birth, marriage, and death, are marked in simple ways that involve the Muslim community. There are no ceremonies or rituals. Social customs surrounding each event may vary from country to country, but the central Islamic practice is the same worldwide.

Birth

The birth of a baby is a happy occasion. Muslims say that a baby is a gift from Allah and brings *barakah* (blessings). The first words a newborn child should hear are those of the *adhan*, which are whispered into his or her right ear. The words of the *iqamah* are spoken into the left ear.

When a baby is about a week old, family and friends are invited to celebrate his or her naming. The *adhan* and the *iqamah* are said again, and a taste of honey may be put on the baby's tongue, to link the sweet words with the sweet taste. The baby's hair may be shaved and the tiny amount of hair weighed on a goldsmith's or pharmacist's scales. The family then makes a gift to charity of the value of the same weight of silver.

Circumcision

Following the sunna of the prophet ﷺ, Muslim boys are circumcised. In some cases this happens in the first few days after birth. In Morocco it is more usual to wait until the boy is four or five and, in Turkey, even ten.

Growing up

By joining in the family religious activities, Muslim children learn to pray, to be clean for prayer, to be

THE ADHAN AND THE IQAMAH

The adhan is the Muslim call to prayer. Each line is said twice, except for the last line which is said once:

Allahu Akbar	Allah is most Great!
Allahu Akbar	Allah is most Great!
Ashhadu an la ilaha illa-Llah	I testify there is no god but Allah.
Asshadu anna Muhammad ar-Rasulullah	I testify that Muhammad is the Messenger of Allah.
Hayyi'ala-s-salah	Hasten to prayer!
Hayyi'alal-falah	Hasten to prosperity!
Allahu Akbar	Allah is most Great!
La ilaha illa-llah	There is no god but Allah.

The *iqamah* is the call to stand up for prayer. It is the same as the *adhan* except that, after *Hayyi'alal-falah*, these words are said twice:

Qad qamat as-salah	Prayer has started.

modest, and to understand the basics of Islam. From an early age they learn to read the Koran, at home or at a local *madrasah* or at a mosque. From when they are seven, their parents must tell them to pray at the five prayer times.

After puberty, young people are responsible for carrying out Islamic practices, including performing *salah* five times daily and fasting during the whole month of Ramadan. Schools with pupils from a variety of faiths often set aside a room where Muslim pupils can pray at lunchtime and in the late afternoon in winter.

Teachers in these schools are sometimes worried that it is unhealthy for young people to fast. Neither Islam nor Muslim parents are cruel. Young people come to no harm when they

Muslim children in Kashgar, western China

37

fast during Ramadan, as long as they eat nourishing meals at night and before dawn.

Also, after puberty, many Muslim girls start wearing the *hijab* (head scarf) whenever they go out of their home. In non-Muslim countries this requires particular courage and commitment, because wearing the *hijab* often attracts adverse comments and bad treatment.

Marriage

Wedding customs differ around the Muslim world. Weddings can take place at home, in mosques, or in community centers. Some Muslim brides wear local costume and lots of jewelry, while others wear white. A Muslim marriage must be publicly announced and celebrated, so the occasion may last several days and take place in different locations, with bride and groom needing a variety of outfits.

The hijab *is a head scarf large enough to cover the neck and chest. It is not a face-covering veil. All Muslims must dress modestly, in loose-fitting, nontransparent clothes. They wear styles suitable for their occupations and for the climates and cultures of the places in which they live.*

The actual wedding, the *nikkah*, is simple and can be performed by any Muslim man at any time. There must be two adult male witnesses of good character, plus a *wali*—the bride's marriage guardian, usually a male relative. A marriage contract will have been prepared. It states that the groom will provide *mahr*, a sum of money as a gift, to the bride. If any special conditions have been included in the contract, such as where the couple have agreed to live, these must be announced. The couple accepts the contract in front of the witnesses. Some words of advice are spoken, and prayers are said for the happiness of the marriage.

The bridegroom's family gives a feast called *walimah*. Guests bring gifts and wish the couple well. Marriage unites the families of the bride and groom and obliges them to help, advise, and support the couple.

At a wedding in Tashkent, Uzbekistan

Hajj

Once in a lifetime, if they have the health and the means, Muslims must make the hajj—the pilgrimage to Mecca, Mina, Muzdalifah, and Arafat.

ON HAJJ

"Last year I went on hajj with my mother, father, and sister. When we first went into the big mosque at Mecca and saw the Kaaba, we all cried with happiness. We did *tawaf*, walking around the Kaaba seven times, and *sa'y*. One day we got separated from my dad and it took ages to find him because all the men looked so alike in their *ihram*.

"On the 8th of Dhul Hijjah we went to Mina, five miles outside Mecca, and slept overnight there before setting off for Arafat. Many people walked the whole eight miles, because the roads got jammed with buses. We tried to get close to where the prophet ﷺ gave his last speech, and we spent the day in prayer. On our way back we camped at Muzdalifah, and collected 49 small stones each from the desert.

"The 10th was *Id* day! After praying *Fajr*, we hurried back to Mina and each threw seven stones at the largest of the three pillars that represent the devils. Everyone cut a lock of hair and some men shaved their heads, and then we went back to Mecca to do *tawaf* again. It was a very hectic day! Back in Mina, we changed out of *ihram* into our ordinary clothes.

"On the 11th and again on the 12th we stoned all three pillars. Some people had to be reminded to throw carefully. Then we returned to Mecca.

"On hajj I forgot about everything else—school, home, sports. Being on hajj put Allah at the center of everything. When I came back to Munich, all my friends said I had changed. They said I was more kind and not so sarcastic." (Hasan Dyke, Germany, age 12)

Tents at Mina for pilgrims

In the past, the journey to hajj could take months or years. Today pilgrims from all over the world fly to Jeddah and travel on to Mecca. Before leaving, all business must be put in order and each person must make his or her will.

Male pilgrims wear two unsewn pieces of white cloth and many women choose to wear all-white clothes. Everything that pilgrims do on hajj reenacts events in the lives of the prophets Ibrahim, Isma'il, and Muhammad. For example, *sa'y* means walking seven times between the hills of Safa and Marwah, in memory of how Hajar, the wife of Ibrahim ﷺ, ran between them, searching for water for her baby son, Isma'il ﷺ.

Three stone pillars at Mina represent devils who tried to tempt the prophet Isma'il ﷺ to disobey his father Ibrahim ﷺ and Allah. Isma'il ﷺ threw stones at the devils, and in remembrance of this, Muslim pilgrims throw stones at the pillars.

Muslim graves are dug so that, when the body is placed on its right side, the deceased faces Mecca.

Death

When a Muslim is dying, people encourage him or her to say the *Shahadah*. And when Muslims hear about someone's death, they say: "To Allah we belong and to Him is our return" (Koran 2:156).

After death, the body is thoroughly washed, not fewer than three times. A man's body is then shrouded in three pieces of white cloth, and a woman's in five. Often the body is taken to a mosque, where the imam or a knowledgeable person chosen by the family says the funeral prayer. As soon as possible, preferably within 24 hours of death, the body is buried. For three days after the burial, and in Turkey and Iran on the seventh and fortieth days, friends bring food to help the mourning family and gather in their house to pray and read the Koran. This comforts and supports them.

7

THE ISLAMIC YEAR

The most important festivals in the Islamic year are *Id ul-Fitr* and *Id ul-Adha*. These were celebrated during the lifetime of the Prophet Muhammad ﷺ. Sunni and Shiite Muslims celebrate these festivals.

The chart on the next page shows events that Muslims remember through the year. Sunni Muslims commemorate events that are related in the Koran and events in the life of the prophet Muhammad ﷺ. In addition, Shiite Muslims offer special prayers on the dates of birth and death of all the immediate family of the prophet ﷺ.

A mosque in Malaysia, lit up to celebrate the joyful occasion of Id

THE BIRTHDAY OF FATIMAH ZAHRAH

Al-Zahrah school in London is named after Fatimah Zahrah, the daughter of the Prophet Muhammad ﷺ. One year on *Yawm al-Zahrah*, the birthday of Fatimah Zahrah, the girls put on a special event for their mothers. They sang songs and told stories about Fatimah Zahrah. Many of the songs were in Arabic, but some were in English. A videotape of the whole celebration was made to sell to families to raise funds for the school.

One story of Fatimah Zahrah tells of how the prophet Muhammad ﷺ was praying at the Kaaba when some men threw garbage on him. Fatimah stood up to them and told them off; she was only nine years old. The girls at the London school had written poems about this, saying how much they would like to be like Fatimah.

THE ISLAMIC CALENDAR

Muslims worldwide use a lunar calendar. The months are based on the sighting of the new moon. They are:

Muharram
Safar
Rabi'al-Awwal
Rabi'al-Thani
Jumada al-Awwal
Jumada al-Thani
Rajab
Sha'ban
Ramadan
Shawal
Dhul Qad'ah
Dhul Hijjah

A lunar year is about eleven days shorter than the solar 365-day year. Therefore events in the Islamic year fall on different dates in the solar calendar every year.

Month and date		Event
Muharram	1	Hegira (Migration)
	10	Ashura
Rabi' al-Awwal	12-17	Maulid an-Nabi
Jumada al-Awwal	15	The Birthday of Zayn al-Abidin
Jumada al-Thani	20	Yawm al-Zahrah
Rajab	27	Laylat ul-Isra wal Mi'raj
Sha'ban	14-15	Laylat ul-Barat
Ramadan		The month of fasting
	23-27	Laylat ul-Qadr
Shawal	1	Id ul-Fitr
Dhul Hijjah	8-10	The Hajj
	10-12	Id ul-Adha

THE ISLAMIC YEAR

What it Commemorates	What Happens
The prophet Muhammad ﷺ moves to Medina, 622 C.E., and establishes first Islamic state. Islamic calendar calculated from this date.	Islamic year begins.
The martyrdom of Imam Hussein ﷺ in Kerbala, Iraq, 680 C.E.	People fast during daylight hours and retell the events.
The birth, life, and example of Muhammad ﷺ. Because Sunni and Shiite Muslims acknowledge different dates for the birth, the 12th and 17th, the week between is used to promote Islamic unity.	People meet to recite Sirah, the Prophet's ﷺ biography, give thanks to Allah for the Prophet ﷺ and his good example, and encourage love for the Prophet ﷺ.
Great-grandson of the prophet ﷺ and son of Imam Hussein ﷺ. He wrote a beautiful book of prayers.	
The birthday of Fatimah Zahrah, daughter of the prophet Muhammad ﷺ and mother of Imam Hussein ﷺ. She is known as the leader of women.	Shiite Muslims encourage love of Fatimah and the following of her good example with poems and stories about her life. In Iran, this day is also commemorated as women's or mother's day.
The Night Journey of the prophet Muhammad ﷺ (see page 9).	People make efforts to say extra prayers at night.
The Night of Promises, when Allah decides what will happen to all of His creation in the coming year.	People make extra efforts to pray for forgiveness and in gratitude and hope for the future.
As ordered by Allah in the Koran. Gives a special sense of community.	People fast from food, drink, and other normally permitted actions from before dawn to sunset every day for the whole month.
The Night of Power (see page 9). It is a hidden night, looked for in the last ten days of Ramadan.	Extra prayers are said during these nights. People thank Allah for His guidance.
Festival to mark the start of the new month and the end of fasting.	People attend *Id* prayers at the mosque and give *zakah* (*zakat-ul-Fitr*) to ensure everyone can join the festivities. They visit family and friends.
Events in the life of the prophets Ibrahim, Isma'il, and Muhammad as ordered in the Koran.	Muslims must make the hajj at least once in their lives.
The Feast of Sacrifice, which is part of the hajj.	An animal may be sacrificed. People attend *Id* prayers at the mosque.

Some people do not have to fast. They are the old and frail; children who have not reached puberty; people who are sick or recovering from illness; pregnant women and nursing mothers; and people who are traveling from one place to another.

"But if anyone is ill or on a journey, the prescribed period should be made up by days later. Allah intends every facility for you: He does not want to put you to difficulties. [He wants you] to complete the prescribed period and to glorify Him." (Koran 2:184)

Ramadan

Ramadan is the ninth month of the Islamic year. It was in Ramadan that the Koran was first revealed to Muhammad ﷺ, and it was during this month each year that the revelations were checked.

Ramadan is the month of fasting, ordered by Allah in the Koran:

O you who believe! Fasting is prescribed to you as it was prescribed to those before you that you may learn self-restraint. (Koran 2:183)

Each day during the 29 or 30 days of the month, from before dawn until sunset, Muslims fast from food, drink, and other normally permitted activities.

RAMADAN IN MEDINA

Muslims from all over the world try to spend Ramadan in Mecca and Medina, the cities where the Koran was revealed. The Prophet's Mosque in Medina is now one of the largest in the world.

After the sunset call to prayer has been made, everyone breaks the fast. People who have brought dates, fruit, and Arabic coffee share them with those near them. People who live in Medina permanently consider it an honor to bring and share food with their fellow Muslims in this way.

Umar Hegedüs from London has been in Medina for several Ramadans. He says, "The atmosphere in the Prophet's Mosque in Ramadan is very special. You feel very close to the Muslim *ummah* and to the ideals of sharing that began with the first Islamic community."

They feel hungry and thirsty, but most Muslims enjoy Ramadan because it brings the community together in a positive way. Someone who is fasting in the heat of west Africa knows that Muslims in cold places like Finland and western China are fasting, too. Fasting reminds people of how they are dependent on Allah, so it gives them greater *taqwa* (consciousness of Allah).

Praying behind the sheikh in Ramadan, Peckham, England

RAMADAN IN LONDON

The Yeni Peckham Cami, the New Peckham Mosque, is a complete contrast with the Prophet's Mosque in Medina. It is a converted church building. But here, too, members of the local Muslim community share their meals with visitors from overseas. Every year in Ramadan, the Turkish-run mosque is host to Sheikh Muhammad Nazim, a Sufi Sheikh (see Glossary). He comes to help Muslims living in a non-Muslim country to observe all the practices of Ramadan. He is a well-known and respected teacher, so his pupils (*murids*) come from all over the world to spend Ramadan with him. Every afternoon, when it is most difficult to fast, Sheikh Nazim talks to his *murids*. He teaches them that, wherever they are from—Malaysia, Canada, Germany, Australia, Pakistan, Scotland, Cyprus, or France—they are all one *ummah*; and the teachings of the Koran can be practiced wherever they live.

It was a custom in Egypt to use special lamps to light the way to the mosque for night prayers. Now they are often carried by children as part of the fun of Ramadan.

Glossary

adhan	Call to prayer, made five times a day from the mosque, in the home, or wherever people make *salah*.	*ihram*	1. The state or condition Muslims enter into to perform hajj and *umrah*. Many normally permitted actions are temporarily forbidden. 2. The name of the two plain white unsewn cloths worn by male pilgrims, indicating brotherhood, equality, and purity. For women the dress of *ihram* consists of their normal modest clothing.
Allah	The Islamic name for the One True God in the Arabic language. Used in preference to the word God, the term has no plural and no gender characteristics.		
ayatollah	A religious leader among Shiite Muslims.		
hajj	Annual pilgrimage to Mecca, in the month of Dhul Hijjah, which each Muslim must undertake at least once in a lifetime. A Muslim male who has completed hajj is called hajji (feminine: hajjah). See also *umrah*.	*imam*	Literally, "leader;" a person who leads communal prayer or a founder of an Islamic school of law. In Shia Islam, imam is also the title of Ali ﷺ and his successors.
halal	Any action that is permitted or lawful.	*iqamah*	Call to stand up for *salah*.
haram	Anything forbidden or unlawful.	**Islam**	Peace attained through willing obedience to Allah's divine guidance.
hijab	Literally, "curtain" or "veil;" often used to describe the head scarf or modest dress for women, who must cover everything except their faces and hands when in the sight of anyone other than their immediate family.	*khutbah*	Speech made on special occasions, such as the Friday and *Id* prayers.
		minbar	Platform from which the imam delivers the *khutbah* in the mosque or praying ground.
Hegira	The emigration of the prophet Muhammad ﷺ from Mecca to Medina in 622 C.E.	**Muhammad**	Literally, "praised;" the name of the final prophet.
Id	Literally, "recurring happiness;" a religious holiday for thanking Allah and celebrating a happy occasion.	**Muslim**	One who claims to have accepted Islam by professing the *Shahadah*.
Id ul-Adha	Celebration of the Sacrifice—commemorating the Prophet Ibrahim's willingness to sacrifice his son Isma'il for Allah.	*salah*	Prescribed communication with and worship of Allah, performed under specific conditions, in the manner taught by the Prophet Muhammad ﷺ and recited in the Arabic language. The five daily times of *salah* are fixed by Allah.
Id ul-Fitr	Celebration of breaking the fast the day after Ramadan ends, the first of Shawal, the tenth Islamic month.		

sawm	Fasting from just before dawn until sunset. Abstinence is required from all food and drink (including water), smoking, and conjugal relations.
Shahadah	Declaration of faith, which consists of this statement: "There is no god except Allah, and Muhammad is the messenger of Allah."
Shari'ah	Islamic law based on the Koran and sunna.
sheikh	A respected person who knows a great deal about Islam and about how to lead a good life and who teaches these things to others.
Sirah	Biographical writings about the conduct and example of the prophet Muhammad ﷺ.
Sufi	A Muslim who tries to become closer to Allah. Sometimes Muslims do this by meeting to recite the Koran and the names of Allah. Both Sunni and Shiite Muslims can follow the Sufi path.
tawaf	Walking seven times around the Kaaba in worship of Allah. A part of hajj and *umrah*.
ummah	The worldwide Muslim community.
umrah	The lesser pilgrimage to Mecca which can be performed at any time of year.
wudu	Washing before *salah*.
zakah	Purification of wealth by payment of an annual welfare tax. This is an obligatory act of worship. The zakah is used to help people in need.
zakat-ul-Fitr	Welfare payment given before the end of Ramadan.

Book List

The Koran
Most of the extracts from the Koran used in this book are taken from the English translation and commentary by Abdullah Yusuf Ali. Many Muslims think that the style and choice of words of his translation make it close in meaning to the original words revealed to the Prophet Muhammad ﷺ. Yusuf Ali worked for many years translating and giving helpful explanations of difficult passages. His work was published in thirty installments from 1934 to 1937.

Ahmad, Fazi. *Muhammad the Prophet of Islam*. Chicago: Kazi Publications, 1984.

Duckworth, John et al. *Muhammad and the Arab Empire*. San Diego: Greenhaven Press, 1980.

Gordon, Matthew S. *Islam*. New York: Facts on File, 1992.

Husain, Shahrukh. *Mecca*. Holy Cities. New York: Dillon Press, 1993.

Iqbal, Muhammad. *Guiding Crescent*. Chicago: Kazi Publications, 1985.

Iqbal, Muhammad. *The Way of the Muslim*. Chester Springs, PA: Dufour Editions, 1983.

Kernaghan, Pamela. *The Crusades: Cultures in Conflict*. New York: Cambridge University Press, 1993.

Moktefi, Mokhtar. *The Arabs in the Golden Age*. Peoples of the Past. Brookfield, CT: Millbrook Press, 1992.

Morris, Scott E., ed. *Religions of the World*. Using and Understanding Maps. New York: Chelsea House, 1993.

Morrison, Ian A. *The Middle East*. World in View. Milwaukee: Raintree Steck-Vaughn, 1991.

Naff, Alixa. *Arab Americans*. The Peoples of North America. New York: Chelsea House, 1988.

Nasr, Seyyed Hossein. *A Young Muslim's Guide to the Modern World*. Chicago: Kazi Publications, 1993.

Note on Dates

Each religion has its own system for counting the years of its history. The starting point may be related to the birth or death of a special person or an important event. In everyday life, today, when different communities have dealings with each other, they need to use the same counting system for setting dates in the future and writing accounts of the past. The Western system is now used throughout the world. It is based on Christian beliefs about Jesus: A.D. (*Anno Domini* = in the year of our Lord) and B.C. (Before Christ). Members of the various world faiths use the common Western system, but, instead of A.D. and B.C., they say and write C.E. (in the Common Era) and B.C.E. (before the Common Era).

Index